Turning

for

Sunlight

Twenty-One Maxims of Living Wisdom
from
Buddhism and Japanese Psychology
to Cope with Difficult Times

by Gregg Krech

ToDo Institute · www.thirtythousanddays. org · Monkton · VT

Dedicated

to

my oldest daughter

Chani Rose Krech

whose laughter, smile and enthusiasm

make this world a better

place to live.

Published by the ToDo Institute

A 501(c)(3) not for profit organization

PO Box 50 Monkton, VT 05469

(802) 453-4440

www.todoinstitute.org

www.thirtythousanddays.org

The author would like to gratefully acknowledge those individuals whose quotes are used as maxims in this book: Ezra Bayda, Dzigar Kongtrul, Soen Naikagawa Roshi, and Kate Manahan.

Cover image photo by: Falkenpost

Maxim font: *Gloss & Bloom* by Sean Delloro
www.instagram.com/seandllr/

Table of Contents

Introduction

You may remember hearing various slogans or maxims when you were a child. For example, "An apple a day keeps the doctor away" or "a stitch in time saves nine." In my youth, I found certain slogans clever, but not very profound and I rarely paid much attention to them. I never actually sat down to discuss or contemplate their meaning.

Yet there is a long tradition of using such maxims for spiritual training. In Buddhism, one of the oldest examples of this is the *Lojong* text or the *Root Text of the Seven Points of Training the Mind*. The origins of this work can be traced back to the tenth-century Buddhist teacher Atisha, and the fifty-nine slogans it contains were later compiled by Geshe Chekawa Yeshe Dorje. There are numerous books with written commentaries on these slogans by contemporary teachers such as Pema Chodron, Chogyam Trungpa, Norman Fischer, Ken McLeod and Alan Wallace.

The study of such slogans involved more than a superficial examination. They were to be studied and considered in the context of one's life. You weren't simply expected to know them – you were expected to live them.

The maxims I've included in this book are part of a collection which I have used personally and for teaching Japanese Psychology. As you'll see, some of these maxims have been borrowed from others, including several Buddhist teachers whose work I admire and find valuable.

I offer you these maxims, along with my commentaries, in an effort to help you find a bit of sunlight in some of your darker moments. When things are going our way, we're often lax about spiritual practice or searching for new ideas. But when we're struggling the most, we may find ourselves grasping for something, anything, that will help us find our way out of darkness and gloom. So while many of these maxims can be considered and applied even when we feel relaxed and happy, their value will often increase when we're depressed, anxious or struggling with how to navigate a dangerous passage on our journey.

Most of the maxims in this book are extensions of ideas that come from three different models of Japanese Psychology: **Naikan, Morita Therapy,** and **Kaizen**. Naikan is a method of self-reflection which provides a structured approach to stepping back from our lives and helping us to see our "karma" in a way that we usually miss. Morita Therapy is a model of psychology which emphasizes action, purpose, and engagement with the world around us. These two approaches are somewhat reflective of the Japanese concepts of *Tariki* (other-power) and *Jiriki* (self-power).

Kaizen provides a practical and effective way of making changes and moving forward once one has determined a direction. I have written extensively about these approaches in my other books (See Resources) and I encourage you to investigate them more fully.

How to Use This Book for Personal Training

Once you've read this book, you can either set it aside or begin to work with the maxims. I would like to recommend a structured approach to such work, though you are, of course, welcome to modify my suggestions to conform to your own circumstances and inclinations.

After reading the book, go through it again and find one particular maxim that resonates with you most clearly. If you find more than one, just pick one of them. The next step is to visually place the maxim where you will be reminded of it frequently. You can print it and leave it on the toilet seat. You can tape it below your car stereo or on the handle of the refrigerator. You can even make it into a screensaver for your laptop or phone. Quite simply, you are trying to remember the maxim, so you may wish to design clever ways to be reminded.

Then, begin to work with the maxim by bringing it to life as often as you can throughout the day. What does it mean to bring it to life? It means you begin to use it and apply it to various situation and circumstances.

For example, it's the end of my workday on a beautiful, warm summer day here in Vermont. I had planned to drive down to my favorite place on Lake Champlain for a swim, but now I'm feeling tired and lethargic. I feel like lying down on the couch for a nap. I don't feel any "swimming energy." Then I remember the maxim, *Lead with the Body*. So I put on my swimsuit and grab a towel. My body takes action. My mind is whining – "You didn't sleep well at all last night." I feel tired. My body grabs the car keys and I start the car. Once I've driven for about three minutes, my mind gives up its whining. When I

7

arrive at the bay, I really don't feel like getting into the water. Not feeling like it, my body takes the lead. I dive in the water. It's cold. I swim for twenty minutes. I'm refreshed. I exercised. I admire the view of the bay and the sculpted mountains that surround it.

It doesn't always work so well. Sometimes you'll remember the maxim and you'll just ignore it and take a nap. That's OK. Celebrate your successes. If you succeed three out of ten times, you're doing as well as some of the best hitters in professional baseball.

You can work with your favorite maxim for a week and then select another for the next week. There are a total of twenty maxims. If you finish all twenty, you can start over again. In fact, if you go through three cycles it will take you 40 weeks. Then take a week to reflect on your experience and start over again. This time select the ten maxims that are the most challenging for you. Ten more weeks of practice. If you really practice sincerely for 51 weeks, contact me and I'll send you a new maxim for the last week of the year.

Conclusion

As we move through life we are eventually faced with situations that force us to work at our edge. You know you're at your edge when your experience is, "I can't handle this – it's too much." It's not just that you have this thought. It's a whole-body experience. You feel like you're going to collapse or just fall apart from the weight of the challenges you're facing.

These are the times when you have to see your life as your practice. Whatever comes up, that's your practice. If you feel like life is crushing you and you think, "I don't want to use this as practice – I'm being crushed." Then working with that thought, that experience, is your practice.

Good luck and do your best.

Seven Times

Down,

Eight Times Up

Japanese Saying

("Nana korobi ya oki")

Resilience is the art of getting back up. Whether you are a fan of football or not, one thing is very obvious. If you watch the game for even a few minutes, you will notice that players are continually getting knocked to the ground and, almost every time, are getting back up. Sometimes it may take a while. Sometimes they may need help. Sometimes they may get injured and leave the game. But they nearly always get back up.

We all know what it's like to be knocked to the ground. We get sick. We get injured. We have financial problems. Our kids get into trouble at school. We lose our jobs. Loved ones die. It wears you out when you keep getting knocked down. You get frustrated. You get angry. You get tired. And after a while you get so worn out that you don't really feel like getting back up. You don't feel like playing any more. But you get back up for two reasons:

First, your team needs you. Your team may include your kids or your aging parents, your partner, your dog or colleagues at work. Someone is counting on you to stay in the game and play. The second reason you get up is that you're loved. You don't always notice it because it's easy to become preoccupied with how much you hurt. But you are loved . . . by the farmers who grew the food you ate, the mechanic who changed your oil, and the people who maintain the roads. You are loved by the people who watch over your kids at school and their teachers. You're loved by doctors, pharmacists, plumbers, truck drivers, bakers and mailmen. Even though they don't always meet your expectations, they are doing what they can to try to keep you in the game. Without them the game would be unplayable.

So you're needed and you're loved. And when you get back up — even though you feel worn down and exhausted – you have a great opportunity. You have the chance to show someone else that you need them and love them. And then you can help them up and give them a reason for staying in the game.

That's how you win.

がんばってください！

ganbatte kudasai!

"hang in there and do your best"

Your Experience of Life is not Based on Your Life, but on What You Pay Attention to

Gregg Krech

On a sunny, Sunday morning in April I went on a hike in the Blue Ridge Mountains of Virginia. Winter storms had strewn many trees and limbs across my path, creating unexpected detours. It seemed like I was constantly climbing over tree trunks, or walking around clusters of fallen branches. The further I hiked, the more irritated I became.

When I reached my destination, I recalled the frustration of the hike and all its unexpected obstacles. How much easier my climb would have been had the timber been cut with a chain saw and cleared away. At that moment, I vaguely recalled a point on the trail where the tree had, in fact, been cut and cleared away. So I decided to do some research.

On my descent I counted the number of trees that were obstacles in my path. But I also counted those that had been moved, cut or cleared to make my path easier. The latter required greater concentration. I had to scan the borders of the path for moved branches and the cut ends of logs. At the end of the sample period of time I was shocked. The reality was that during my ascent there were more trees moved and cleared than left blocking my path. Yet it was the obstacles that dominated my memory of the experience.

For many of us, this hike resembles our lives. We notice the obstacles because we have to get around them to proceed. But if we go through life primarily noticing the obstacles and problems, what is our experience? Anger, resentment, disappointment and frustration. Through skillful attention we are able to see reality as it is. And that awareness allows us to feel cared for and loved because we notice that we are cared for and loved.

Life is a Matter of Attention

If You're Discouraged, Encourage Others

Soen Nakagawa Roshi

Most of us face discouragement from time to time. Either we are confused, overwhelmed, or simply feel we lack what it takes to cope successfully with the situation at hand. So now what do we do? We might simply succumb to the despair of the situation and allow it to immobilize us. Or we may look to others – teachers, family members, friends, books – to guide us out of our sense of discouragement. But the Zen teacher Soen Nakagawa offers us a brilliant solution:

Encourage Others!

How can we encourage others when we're discouraged ourselves? Normally we think that there is a person who is discouraged and that person is suffering. And there is another person who provides encouragement. That person is doing well and has his act together. But Nakagawa Roshi says that when we are suffering, that is when we should provide encouragement to others. He doesn't say, "first get yourself together, and then give others encouragement." It's the act of encouraging others that heals our own discouragement.

The secret underlying this process has to do with attention. When we are discouraged, all of our attention is on ourselves. "My life is so hard. I don't have the strength. I'm disappointed and demoralized. I'm overwhelmed." Our attention is glued to our own suffering. But to encourage others, you have to shift your attention to the suffering of the other person. "How is their life hard? What is the nature of their difficulty? How can I support them?" When you shift your attention to encouraging someone else, you have removed the nourishment for your own suffering.

St. Francis' prayer is about shifting one's attention away from oneself. The fact that it's a prayer is testimony to its difficulty. Sometimes we'll succeed and at other times we'll just fall on our face. If you fall on your face often enough, you get discouraged. And then . . .

Grant that I may not

so much seek to be consoled,

as to console.

St. Francis

According to Ilya Prigogine, a physicist who was awarded the Nobel Prize in chemistry, nothing grows without friction. It is a fundamental property of nature that is essential to the growth of everything.

"It is precisely this quality of fragility, the capacity for being shaken up, that is paradoxically the key to growth."

You Can't

Figure Out Life

in

Your Mind

Gregg Krech

W hen you are faced with a predicament or challenge, what do you do? If you're smart then you probably try to think of a solution. You try to *think* your way out of your predicament. Too often we approach life as if it were a chess game.

We try to anticipate a whole string of moves. I'll do this and then life will do this, and then I'll do that, and life will respond by doing that. We create a mental map which ends in our winning — winning being defined as getting the outcome we desire.

But then life doesn't respond the way we expected. Life doesn't play by linear rules. For example, it's your move and life just grabs your bishop. Or life just turns your queen into a pawn. And that leaves you frustrated and disappointed. And exhausted, mentally and emotionally.

We can't play chess with life because life isn't a chess game. We can't think our way through our dilemmas and challenges. We can't count on anything being predictable from one day to the next – from one *hour* to the next.

We need to give up chess and start dancing.

We listen for the music. Feel the beat. Life takes a step, we take a step. Life twirls us, and our task is to twirl as gracefully as possible. We are not trying to outsmart life -- we are trying to be a good partner. Sometimes we lead, sometimes life leads. We try not to step on anyone's toes. And if we trip over our own feet, we laugh at ourselves and get up.

Chess is a game of intensity, of competition, of thinking and more thinking. Dancing is movement — movement without thought.

When you first learn to dance you think about every step: "Now I'll put my left foot here. Now I'll do this with my right foot. After you practice for a while, or dance regularly, you stop thinking about your next move.

Surrender to the music -- whatever happens to be playing at the moment. Dance your way through life.

Life is either your partner, or an opponent. Sometimes life truly feels like an opponent. But if you constantly battle life you get worn out. Of course, you'll also get worn out dancing. But it's a different kind of worn out. At the end of the night, it's more like, "I'm too exhausted to dance one more step . . . but let's do this again."

Show me slowly what I
only know the limits of.
Dance me to the end of love.

-   Leonard Cohen

Take Action in the Midst of Sadness

Gregg Krech

T he great Tibetan Buddhist teacher, Chogyam Trungpa, offers excellent advice on how to move forward in our life even though our hearts might be filled with sadness. His guidance is,

> *"Hold the sadness and pain of samsara in your heart and at the same time the power and vision of the Great Eastern Sun. Then the warrior can make a proper cup of tea."*

The first thing we must do is hold pain and sadness in our hearts. Most of us do this, but not skillfully enough. We are in touch with the disappointment of not getting a promotion, the frustration of our child's drug addiction, or even the gloom that comes from watching the news of all the violence and suffering in the world.

But to hold the sadness and pain in our heart is to be aware of the sadness and pain in our heart.

We notice and acknowledge the feeling of disappointment, gloom, and frustration -- and we hold it in our heart with warmth and tenderness. Think about how you usually respond to the feeling of sadness or depression. You want to get rid of it. You want to avoid it. You want to make it go away.

This is usually why people go to therapy. We want to fix our feelings. That is different than holding our experience in our heart. We meet our sadness with tenderness. We meet our pain with warmth and openness.

The second element of Trungpa's advice is to hold the power and vision of the Great Eastern Sun in our hearts at the same time. Now this is tricky. What is the Great Eastern Sun, anyway? The Great Eastern Sun represents a combination of wisdom and discipline. It is about moving forward. It is about waking up to your life. The Great Eastern Sun shows us what to do and not do. It is cheerful and illuminating.

So we are asked to hold on to the illuminating sun, even as we hold on to our sadness and pain. Is this possible? Can we hold two seemingly opposing views in our heart simultaneously? Don't answer with the word-thoughts of your mind. Try it and see if you can do it.

This morning, I sat on the deck of the ToDo Institute, staring out at a beautiful Vermont valley that was bathed in the morning sun and revealed the hillsides of the rolling Green Mountains. In the background were sounds of bluejays, chickadees and crows. Red squirrels were chattering in the tall pine just above me. There was a gentle breeze coming from the west and the petunia petals in the flower box were dancing ever so slightly.

Yet I am sad. My 83 year-old mother was diagnosed with cancer last week. She lives seven hundred miles away and this morning she is in a nursing facility. She is depressed and lonely. She is refusing treatment and says she wants to die. So I am holding this great sadness in my heart while I am bathing in the morning sun, the songs of the birds and the joy of being surrounded by a wonderful family of my own. I am aware of the impermanence of life and that all things must change. And at the same time I am filled with the pain of my mother's suffering.

The haiku poet, Issa, represents this profound experience in one of his most famous poems:

The world of dew

is the world of dew.

And yet, and yet ...

He wrote this poem after the funeral of his baby daughter. All three of his children died before they reached their first birthday. What great sadness he had to carry in his heart. He understands that this world is impermanent. The "world of dew" is a world of birth and death. The morning dew is here in the morning and gone once it meets the rays of the sun. All things are subject to change. So Issa's recognition of "the world of dew" is a statement of his own realization. He understands the way the world is. But "and yet, and yet" is a statement of his pain. It is the cry of a human being. It reflects his own humanity as a father. In this very short poem, he expresses both his sadness and his wisdom. In this moment, he appears to hold both his grief and the Great Eastern Sun in his tender heart.

There is one final step in Trungpa's advice: *make a proper cup of tea*. Up to this point, everything is about meditation and contemplation. But Trungpa wants us to take action. He wants us to get up and live our life. What is there to do? To make a cup of tea? To feed the birds? To do the laundry? To plan a trip to visit your mother or write a letter to your Senator protesting an injustice? Our heart is filled with both sadness and joy. And we take that heart with us as we act. We move forward with our life and with the awareness that our life (everyone's life) is a bundle of pain and joy.

Pema Chodron, a Buddhist teacher and former student of Chogyam Trungpa, adds a cautionary note to his quote. She says,

"You can be willing to feel fully and acknowledge continually your own sadness and the sadness of life, but at the same time not be drowned in it."

This is the difficulty many of us have when acknowledging our own pain and suffering. We are drowned by it. We lose sight of the Great Eastern Sun and we take no action. Or we act from a heart which is consumed by sadness and depression.

We have a great challenge to meet today. We have to acknowledge our sadness, but also acknowledge the joy, care and blessings of our life, of a world that is also home to daffodils, chickadees and puppies. We have to feel our pain but not be drowned by it. We have to take our sad and joyful heart with us, live our life, and do what is important for us to do. That's asking a lot, isn't it?

Yes, it is.

Our love needs to be bigger than our insanity

Henk Brandt

Gratitude Disappears in the Shadow of Entitlement

Gregg Krech

Whenever you believe you are entitled to something, you are placing it in a shadow. It's like being given a beautiful rosebush and then planting it in the darkest spot in the forest, where it gets no sun. What will happen? Well, eventually it will die. The more we think we deserve something, the more difficult it is to genuinely appreciate it as a gift.

My wife brings me a hot cup of coffee. My daughter fills the car with gas. My colleague sends me a book I might like. If I think I deserve these things, my responses might be:

"It's about time you made the coffee."
"Wow, for once she actually left me a car with gas."
"That's the first time she ever sent me something without my asking for it."

But suppose I start from a different place -- a place where I'm not entitled to anything, where I don't deserve anything.

I'm not entitled to coffee or to drive a car. I don't deserve a nice dinner on my birthday. I don't even deserve a WiFi signal or cell phone service. Suppose you could start your day with a sense that you were entitled to nothing.

Everything, at that point, would truly be received and experienced as a gift. The use of a toilet, hot water in the shower, a toothbrush, the use of a telephone and the roads that allow you to drive to work -- each of these items and experiences is like a rosebush planted in a sunny garden. After a while the whole garden is full of roses.

So here's a trade-in better than any car dealer will ever offer you: trade your sense of self-entitlement for an expanse of roses as far as you can see.

No down payment required. Just daily maintenance.

I Get to . . .

Kate Manahan

Walking the dog. Making dinner. Picking the kids up from school. Doing laundry. We generally think of these tasks as chores – things we need to do, have to do, should do. If you have a family, or a demanding job (or both) you may spend a lot of time doing such tasks. If you can get through your list, you may be able to squeeze in some time for the things you really want to do: yoga, a bike ride, a relaxing bath, or just reading a magazine on the sofa. This is the life of "reluctant action." Much of what occupies our precious time is infused with a psychological and spiritual reluctance.

The maxim, "I Get to . . ." is the antidote to living a reluctant life. I get to walk the dog. I get to wash the dishes. I get to go to the supermarket for food. The phrase *I Get to* implies that it is a privilege to do such activities – a blessing. It's a blessing to be able to put gas in my car. It's a privilege to be able to water the plants.

At first this seems like nothing but a play on words. We simply substitute *I Get to* for *I Have to*. No big deal. But the power of this maxim is in stimulating a reflective pause, an investigation of what we are doing and how it might be more than just a chore or errand.

A few years ago I injured my ankle playing basketball and in the course of one day I went from running up and down a basketball court to being unable to walk up and down my driveway without holding on to my wife's arm. For years I had taken my dog, Barley, down to the road and back up the hill to our house. On many of those days I was busy with my work and I treated that walk as an imposition on my time. There were winter days with subzero temperatures. There were hot, humid days where flies buzzed around my head. But now, unable to walk unaided, I realized that those easy walks were gifts. How lucky I had been to be able to walk up and down my driveway.

I am blessed to be able to put a little, plastic card in a gas pump and drive another 300 miles. I'm blessed to have a store with so many different food items to choose from (and money to purchase them). I get to pick up my daughter from school today. I get to feed the birds. I get to fill out forms for health insurance and college financial aid. I get to live another day.

When it Comes

to Attention,

"I" am the

Enemy

Gregg Krech

Last night the stars put me in my place, just as they have many times in the past. As I wandered down the hillside beneath my home I was accompanied by an old dog and a chatty, scattered mind.

Then I looked up. As soon as I became aware of how big the universe is, I realized how small I am. There were hundreds of glistening stars putting on a show entitled, "You (that's me) are not the center of the universe." Now this is not new information to me. I once asked a former teacher to review a draft manuscript and he commented on how many times I used the word "I" in my writing.

The other day I was driving home behind a red Plymouth driven by an older woman with grey hair. Just when we reached the "Y" in the road before the general store, she went left as I took the road to the right. It suddenly dawned on me that this woman had an entire life that would be continuing at the same time as mine. She had problems, she had aches and pains, she laughed at jokes I had never heard before. How was this possible?

When we begin to study attention seriously, one of the first things we discover is how often our attention is focused on ourselves. Now I'm feeling hungry.

Now thirsty. Now I'm worried about what's going to happen. Now I'm tired. Now I'm looking around the room, not thinking of others, but thinking, "I wonder what they think of me." We notice an item in a store and our reference point is "could really use one of those." We call a business associate to meet for lunch and our primary concern is, "what's most convenient for me." My needs. My wants. My suffering. It's enough to make you sick.

In fact, it does make you sick.

In 1990, psychologist, Rick Ingram reviewed the research that had been done on the subject of self-focused attention. (Psych Bulletin, Vol 107, No.2). This research covered problem areas such as depression, anxiety, alcohol abuse, even schizophrenia. In each case, there was an indication of a direct relationship between self-focused attention and the psychological problem.

"The weight of available data clearly suggests an association between disorder (or vulnerability to disorder) and self-focused attention regardless of the particular disorder," stated Ingram.

Other researchers have drawn similar conclusions. A 1982 study of depression by Jacobson and Anderson found that "depressed people refer to themselves more frequently than do nondepressed people, even when the normal flow of conversation calls for more attention to the other person." (Behavior Therapy, Vol.13). They went on to conclude that "...evidence also seems to suggest that happiness is associated with an outward focus."

Here we have one of the most fundamental and overlooked distinctions in the field of mental health: the contrast between outward attention to the world and attention focused on ourselves. This distinction is a watershed between good and poor mental health; between a healthy, flowing mind and a suffering, self-absorbed one.

Attention, both self-focused and outward, is a skill that we develop in the same way we learn to play the piano. If we practice consistently with the left hand, we become good at playing with our left hand. If we practice with the right, we become good at playing with the right. A good pianist plays well with both hands. However, I have much more dexterity with my right hand than my left. And I'm sorry to report that I have much more dexterity attending to myself than to the world around me. I naturally daydream, plan, worry or do almost anything other than pay attention to what is going on around me at any given moment.

Nearly all of my students echo this self-diagnosis. We are not out of touch with our inner world -- that world of feelings, of preferences, of desires and discomfort. It is a world we know too well. A prison blinds us to a universe of sunsets, spider webs and stars; a universe that is vibrant and breathing with life. The universe wants us to dance, but we are too self-absorbed to hear the invitation.

Every once in a while the beauty of the world around us is so stunning, so captivating that we can no longer ignore it and we forget ourselves and dissolve into something greater. And it's not only beauty which attracts us, it is also need. The needs of a loved one for help, the needs of a community, even a planet.

We find our calling, our bliss, our purposes, by giving up on ourselves. Our surrender becomes our salvation. Our disappearance provides relief, even for a few moments. But once you have tasted those moments you have discovered something about attention. And now you can travel through the world and seek out what isn't so obvious. The shadows of birches late in the afternoon. A weed growing in the fissure of a large boulder. The texture of a rose petal against your cheek. You are on your way to becoming a poet.

The tragedy of traditional psychology that it is still preoccupied with self-preoccupation. Too often, it teaches us to do what we already do too well -- pay attention to ourselves. In the course of exploring our pain, our worries, our feelings and our dreams, we forego the development of our more needed skill -- to notice and engage the world around us. Without practice, our muscles atrophy.

So the next time you find yourself self-absorbed, take a walk. Look around you. The world is an interesting place. It might even give you something to do. If the stars are out, close your eyes. Listen. You might just hear them twinkle.

That is how they get your attention.

Don't Avoid What You Don't Like

Gregg Krech

e tend to move toward what we are attracted to.

"I think I'll have another piece

of that pecan pie."

We tend to move away from what we have an aversion to.

"Thank you, but I think I'll pass on the beets tonight."

Sometimes we have an aversion to what we need to do. So we find all kinds of creative ways to avoid doing what we know needs doing.

Avoidance has a kind of diabolical quality to it: The more we avoid something, the greater our anxiety or fear of it. Our aversion grows. Our anxiety grows. Time passes. Not doing what we need to do has consequences and those consequences can be unpleasant.

The "thing we didn't do" haunts us. It stalks us. Eventually the whole story becomes a scary movie -- maybe even with zombies in it.

We must learn to approach what we have an aversion to. We must learn to attend to what makes us uncomfortable. We need not avoid what we don't like, simply because we don't like it.

The first thing to know is that it's possible to act while having feelings of fear, anxiety, boredom, shyness, disinterest, frustration or any other feeling which accompanies an aversion to the task at hand.

In fact, we do this all the time. We feel sleepy and get out of bed. We lack confidence and try something new for the first time. We crave something sweet but don't eat it. We feel bored, yet we complete our tax return. In essence, we take our feelings along for the ride while we do what needs to be done.

Work with the

Conditons You

Encounter

Gregg Krech

Janet Lipner had a realization recently. She attended a tree care program and, after being certified, she helped to plant trees. She noticed all the factors that help a tree grow: depth and circumference of the hole, soil quality, water, etc. Yet, wherever you plant the tree, the tree has to deal with whatever conditions are present in that location. This is true of any kind of plant, since they cannot move or change their circumstances. Still, the tree doesn't complain about its situation saying,

"I should have been planted in a better spot; now I can't grow well."

The tree does its best with what it has.

It's easy for us to focus on how we were dealt a lousy hand in life and use that as a constant source of complaint and excuse as to why we haven't done better. Such an attitude contributes to our own suffering and to the suffering of others. In fact, by complaining we create conditions for the "trees" around us that make their lives more difficult. So perhaps we can take a lesson from our friends, the trees, and simply do our best with whatever situation we encounter.

The conditions of our lives will always be less than ideal. But just to be planted on this earth for a brief period of time is truly a gift that we should continuously reflect on.

For today, just try to work with the conditions you encounter in your life. You won't be able to get life to conform to your wishes. Your strength and wisdom are measured by your ability to adapt to life. Do what you need to do, given the less than ideal, challenging, not-what-you-wanted circumstances.

Work with the situation instead of fighting it, resisting it, and complaining about it. Save all that energy and use it for something worthwhile.

Deciding

is not

Doing

Gregg Krech

Have you ever been in a quandary and, after considering different options and possibilities, decided what you need to do? This often happens to me. I have to decide on a title for my new book. I have to decide which flight to take for a conference I'm attending.

There are some decisions that are extremely important and require a fair amount of consideration. Trying to decide on the proper software platform and design for a website is clearly important. I remember when we were trying to decide whether to adopt a child. *That decision* had a dramatic effect on my entire life.

But we shouldn't confuse deciding with acting. If you were to watch me making decisions, mostly you would see me

Just Sitting There.

I might be looking something up on the Internet or surveying the grounds, but what you would see me doing is really . . not very much.

And -- this is critical -- the difference in reality before and after the decision is . . .

No Difference.

Until I actually take some constructive action, I have not changed the reality of my life or the world around me at all by just deciding. So please be cautious about thinking of decision-making as something you did. Generally, it's something you thought.

Once you take the first step, then you send ripples into the world.

Lead

with the

Body

Gregg Krech

A central principle of Morita Therapy is that we have much more control over the body (actions) than the mind (feelings/thoughts). During long meditation periods I would find that my mind would be all over the place –

"I wonder what's for lunch today?"

"I wish I would have slept better last night."

Nevertheless, I could keep my body relatively still during the same period. Off the cushion, I've found that I could eat a bowl of beet soup (beets are one of my least favorite foods) even as my mind was saying, "Yuck, beets are totally disgusting."

When you're angry, you can have the thought, "I'm going to strangle this person," and not actually attack them. We don't realize how much control we have over our body, because we don't pay much attention to how often the content of our mind is out of sync with our actions. If we acted on every thought or feeling we had, our lives would be utter chaos (compared to normal chaos).

Of course, you can't always control the body, particularly if your body is medically or physically incapable of a particular action. No amount of willpower will allow me to jump six feet in the air from a standing start.

Yet in many cases, my body is able to do what my mind doesn't want to do or believes it cannot do. Rather than go through a period of mental gymnastics attempting to get the mind to change its mind, we can simply let the body take the lead. We can put on our running shoes even as the mind is thinking,

"I'm way too tired to go for a run."

We can gather our cooking supplies even as the mind thinks,

"I don't feel like cooking – I'll just order a pizza."

We can pull out the file with our tax information while the mind is thinking,

"Forget taxes, I'm just going to see what's happening on Facebook."

Our bodies have much more capacity and power than we give them credit for. So when you notice that your mind is lazy or uncooperative just put your body in charge for a while. And take your mind along for the ride.

Details

Make Life

Interesting

Gregg Krech

Life becomes interesting through the exploration of life's details. Talk to a baker and he may have intimate knowledge of flour. Talk to a master gardener and she'll describe the varieties of tomato plants and the intricacies of growing them. A concert pianist performing at Lincoln Center may go to the Steinway Piano factory and try 14 different grand pianos before selecting one for the concert.

To really pay attention to details we have to use as many of our senses as possible. Too often, we limit ourselves to our visual sense. By using our other senses, as well, we often have a much richer experience.

Think about eating a piece of rich, dark chocolate. We first look at the chocolate. Then we may smell that distinct chocolate aroma with a deep inhalation. And finally we put it into our mouth and feel both the texture as well as the flavor. *(Are you getting hungry yet?)*

When we engage with life using our senses, in great detail, we are pulled out of our ruminations and right into the present moment. We have a moment in which we forget our financial problems or the argument we had earlier in the day. This is sometimes referred to as "distraction" – and that term more often has a negative connotation than a positive one. But distraction is actually a healthy skill. It's the opportunity to shift our attention from being preoccupied with our thoughts, feelings, plans and worries to appreciating and engaging with life in this very moment.

As the Zen teacher, Jan Chosen Bays, says,

"We move from thinking to experiencing."

The world is full of miracles ranging from autumn maple leaves to water polished pebbles on the shore of the ocean. These miracles are available to us if we take the time to pay attention.

In detail.

Respond

to the

Needs

of the

Situation

Gregg Krech

Y ou open the refrigerator door. There are three dishes on the second shelf that catch your eye: a cup of lentil soup, a bowl of salad, and a piece of peach pie. The question we naturally ask without any awareness is usually – *"What do I feel like eating?"*

This simple event, which may happen many times each day, is a clue to how we get ourselves into trouble. We use our feelings as the primary measure of what we choose and don't choose to do. If we feel like having pie, we eat pie. If we feel like having soup, we eat soup. If we feel like having a gin and tonic, we have a drink.

We have, unknowingly, established our feelings as the director of our life's play. And everyone listens to the director. Because we are responding to our feelings, we often get some temporary pleasure. But it's only temporary. We feel like eating pie. We eat the pie. Then here comes this thought,

"You shouldn't have eaten that pie. Can't you stay on your diet for even one day? You have no self-control at all."

Now how do we feel? Rotten? Guilty? Upset?

The alternative is not to kick your feelings out of the play. The alternative is to make them an actor. They have a role to play. Sometimes it's an important role, and sometimes they function as an "extra."

So now who is the director? Let's give that job to *the Needs of the Situation*.

You're taking a walk and spot an empty, dirty beer can. What do you do? You don't feel like picking it up. Let's ask the director – what are the needs of the situation?

Your taxes are due in three days. You'd rather watch a movie. What are the needs of the situation?

Making the needs of the situation the director shifts the focus from preoccupation with our feelings to serving reality. In essence, we respond to life, rather than react to our feelings. How do we determine the needs of the situation?

Just ask.

Not

Happening

Now

Ezra Bayda

What would you estimate is the percentage of time your mind gives to the present moment of your life, compared to the imaginary or substitute life which your mind creates? Would you say it is a 50/50 allocation? Or do you spend a majority of time in your head not really paying attention to the world that exists around you in the present moment? If you do, you can join a very popular club. The membership in that club soars during times of stress, anxiety, confusion and panic.

I was in the car the other day driving through the White Mountains of New Hampshire on my way to a speaking engagement in Maine. I tried to reach my wife at work with a simple, practical question. No answer. I tried the home number and her cell phone. I also tried my daughter's cell phone since I assumed she would be with my wife. No answer anywhere.

At first I thought it was nothing to be concerned about. But my mind had a different idea. It began creating various scenarios explaining what was going on. After a second call, 15 minutes later, which also produced no response, my mind used the uncertainty of the situation as fuel for creating more imaginary and upsetting scenarios.

I remembered this maxim, used by Zen teacher Ezra Bayda, "Not Happening Now." I realized that the only thing that was happening was my dialing the phone and getting a voice mail recording. What *was* actually happening right now?

I began narrating to myself: "There's a sign with the number 70, in black, on a white background, indicating the speed limit. There's a Toyota in front of me with the license plate AR98573. There are numerous pines along the perimeter of the highway and a few maples here and there. I began grounding myself in reality instead of being swept away by illusion. To do this, I had to start by recognizing what's not happening now. I had to come back to reality, to the reality of life here and now.

And I had to accept the uncertainty of the situation. I know there's an exit ramp for Gorham, NH in one mile. I don't know where my wife is at the moment.

We spoke about an hour later. She was fine. Everything was fine. The speed limit was now 65mph. Mt. Washington rose majestically into a blue, summer sky.

Three kinds of souls, three prayers:

1. *I am a bow in your hands, draw me lest I rot;*
2. *Do not overdraw me, I shall break;*
3. *Overdraw me and who cares if I break!*

Nikos Kazantzakis

Examine Life Outside the Boundaries of Your Suffering

Gregg Krech

Ironically, the occasions of our greatest focus are often when we are suffering. We may be struggling with an illness, a layoff, the death of a loved one, or a flat tire. At such times we are often aware of our pain with the precision of a laser beam. Our attention is drawn to our grief, our sadness, our disappointment. We are absorbed into the misfortune that is upon us.

While our attention is restricted to the burden we are trying to bear, we often fail to see the many ways life is caring for us, even trying to help us extricate ourselves from the difficulties we're facing.

How could life be offering us care or support? This is the same life that gave us cancer, or betrayal, or financial disaster. Haven't you done enough? Stay away from me and let me twist and turn in the cobwebs of my adversity.

But life hasn't done enough. It shows up in the form of a doctor. Or medicine. Or a spare tire and jack. It magically appears as electricity or a hot shower. When we're out of work, someone offers us a temporary job or a loan. After our accident we somehow acquire a neck brace or crutches.

Just because we don't feel loved doesn't mean we aren't loved. Just because we don't feel cared for doesn't mean we aren't cared for. We have to look up. We have to look around us and behind us. Sometimes we just have to look right in front of us. Life has not forsaken us. *Don't mistake pain for abandonment.*

When you are weighed down by your challenges, when you find yourself collapsing and gasping for spiritual breath -- look for the sometimes quiet, hidden or taken-for-granted ways that life is supporting you. It means a temporary shift of attention from pain toward love. That shift of attention won't necessarily rescue you from your problems. But it will remind you that you're not alone.

Find Compassion for Others in Your Own Transgressions

Gregg Krech

There is an element of human nature that is poised to judge others as soon as they fall short of our expectations or ideals. How could she do such a thing? How could he treat me like that? We look down from a pedestal of innocence or self-justification. As we grow older, most of us hope that our hearts will soften, but often they are as hard as granite. They harden whenever we condemn people from a position of arrogance, superiority or self-righteousness.

The antidote to a hard heart requires courage and sincerity. It requires us to remember our own human weakness and faults. A sincere self-examination makes it possible to soften our hearts towards others because we become familiar with our own transgressions. And when those transgressions rest in the center of our hearts we can't help but bring the light of understanding and compassion to others. We encounter the faults of others as fellow sinners. And we recognize that our ability to transcend our misdeeds is the result of grace – grace which includes the love, support and guidance of others.

Our minds have developed the capacity to justify ourselves, while we criticize others for the same acts. If we cut someone off in the next lane, we excuse ourselves with the thought, "Oh, I didn't see that car." But when someone cuts us off, we react with, "Hey, you jerk, watch where you're going – you could kill someone." Can you notice the tricks your ego has mastered to make you look good and others look bad? Do you have the courage to bring compassion to the faults of others, as well as yourself?

Like a drifting cloud,

bound by nothing,

I just let go,

giving myself up

to the whim of

the wind

Ryokan

Loosen

Your

Grip

Gregg Krech

This world is out of control. That is, it's out of your control. Consider all the elements of your own life that you can't control. You can't control the weather. You can't control the economy. You can't control natural disasters. You can't control the behavior of anyone you know: your aging parents, your intimate partner, your colleagues at work, your friends, even your children. You can exercise and eat healthy food, but you can't control whether you get a cold or a serious illness. There are traffic delays, plane delays, and cancelled appointments. Much of life is outside your personal control.

When life doesn't go according to our desires and preferences, how do we respond? Often we respond by trying harder to control what we can't control. We tighten our grip. Sometimes this works, but most of the time it doesn't. Trying harder and harder to control what you can't control can simply leave you in a state of tension, frustration, disappointment, and even anger.

The Japanese psychiatrist, Shoma Morita, asked us to embrace the concept of *Arugamama* – meaning to "accept things as they are." Acceptance is the alternative to control. It means we are able to let things be the way they are instead of trying to make them the way we want them to be. This is particularly relevant to the people in our network of friends and family. We see people who are struggling and we want to help them. Our intentions may be noble, but no matter how much we think we know what they should do, we usually can't get them to change. We devote ourselves to fixing them rather than loving them.

Even the inner world of our thoughts and feelings is mostly uncontrollable. We can't control feeling anxious about our kids. We can't control feeling upset about a loved one who is dying. We can't control the stream of distracting thoughts that arise in our mind when we're working or meditating.

A lot of life is uncontrollable. So loosen your grip. You don't have to orchestrate everything. Give things room to grow, wilt, revive and fail. Even your heart has found a way to keep its beat without your vigilant efforts.

Ichi Go, Ichi E

(One time, one meeting)

chi Go Ichi E is a Japanese phrase that literally means "one time, one meeting." However it is often translated as "once in a lifetime encounter." What does this mean?

When I was invited to conduct a series of workshops at a Yoga Center in the Bahamas, I didn't know what to expect. I had probably done yoga twice in sixty years. I went to my first class, a two hour introductory class taught by a wonderful man named Arjuna. He asked if there was anyone who was attending the class for the first time. I raised my hand. It was a wonderful class and I went again the following morning.

Since people come and go at the center, he asked, again, if there was anyone taking the class for the first time. I raised my hand.

I went to the same class every day that week. And every day I raised my hand. In fact, I began doing a weekly class after I returned to Vermont. When I was invited, a year later, to conduct workshops at the same center, I gratefully returned and found myself on the same platform one morning with 32 other people getting ready to do yoga and with Arjuna as the teacher. And when he asked if anyone was taking the class for the first time I raised my hand. He looked at me and laughed. He doesn't speak Japanese, but he understood "ichi go, ichi e." I had taken nearly 50 yoga classes at that point . . . but never this class. This class, these people around me, this day, this teacher – this was a once in a lifetime encounter.

The phrase, ichi go ichi e, can be traced by to Ii Naosuke (1815 -1860) who was chief administrator of the Tokugawa Shogunate and was a highly esteemed tea master. During this time in Japan there was growing tension amongst Japan's leaders related, in part, to pressure from the American consul, Townsend Harris, to finalize a treaty with Japanese authorities. Naosuke would make and drink tea every morning, in the tradition of the Japanese tea ceremony (shado). Naosuke elaborated on the idea of ichi go ichi e when he wrote:

"Even though the host and guests may see each other often socially, one day's gathering can never be repeated exactly. Viewed this way, the meeting is indeed a once-in-a-lifetime occasion. The host, accordingly, must in true sincerity take the greatest care with every aspect of the gathering . . . the guests, for their part, must understand that the gathering cannot occur again and, appreciating how the host has flawlessly planned it, must also participate with true sincerity."

Naosuke knew that threats had been made on his life. When he drank tea, he experienced it as if it was his last time to drink a cup of tea. On March 24, 1860, seventeen retainers from Mito, assisted by Arimura Jisaemon, a samurai from Satsuma, intercepted Naosuke's entourage on the on his way to Edo Castle and killed him.

His dramatic death leaves us with the principle of "once in a lifetime encounter," whether we are drinking coffee, tea, having lunch with a friend, or playing tennis. It's unlikely that we will be assassinated by a samurai later that day. But even if we live, we will never experience that encounter again. Indeed, each encounter has its own unique karmic conditions and we should pour ourselves into the experience the same way Naosuke poured tea on the last day of his life.

If we live with this spirit, we don't hold anything back. We give ourselves and the full force of our being to each encounter as if it were our last. Because it is our last.

Make Yourself

at Home

in the

Unknown

Dzigar Kongtrul

W e are most at home in our own home. We have arranged everything according to our preferences. And when we come home from the movie theater or dinner at a friend's, we know exactly where everything is. Because we feel at home in our home, we also give ourselves permission to relax. We may leave our socks on the floor or an unwashed glass by the sink. For many of us, even if our home is simple, or small, it represents comfort and security.

Last year my teenage daughter and I arrived in Naples, Italy. We had never been there before and had no idea what to expect. We didn't know the layout of the city. We didn't know where to eat. We didn't speak Italian. We found the train station and took a train to the ruins at Pompeii. When we got off the train, we had no idea which way to walk. Everything we saw was new and unexpected. When you go on a trip like this, you can have an adventure, because wherever you go is the unknown. So you become curious, attentive, interested, and open to new experiences.

Yet each day of our life is really unknown, even if we are at home or going to work. We don't know what's going to happen. We don't know what surprises await us. We don't truly know how the day will unfold. If we could view each day as an adventure, we could naturally become curious, attentive, interested and open to new experiences. But, too often, our experience is just the opposite. We encounter something unexpected and we become tense, stressed and uncomfortable.

If we can think of our home as something beyond the building we live in we might be able to relax into our adventure like it was a trip to Naples or Pompeii. Our life is like a mystery novel. *What will happen next? We don't know!* Let's just sit back and see what the next page will reveal. Let's find a way to enjoy life without knowing how the story will end.

Okagesama

If you look around you in your home or office you will probably see walls. Many walls are very smooth and painted. In fact, if your wall is painted, you are really just looking at paint -- you can't really see the wall. But what's inside the wall? Have you ever seen or walked through a home that is under construction or being renovated? If you have, you may have seen the inside of a wall before it is closed up and painted.

Important things are inside your walls. First, there are electrical wires. Wherever you see an electrical outlet, it means that there are wires that run all the way to the source of your electricity, like a system of nerves that travel through your body. Because these wires are placed inside the walls you can't see them, but they allow you to plug in a lamp, or a toaster or a television. Also, most walls are built around the structure of wooden studs. These pieces of wood, when nailed together skillfully, make the walls strong which allows them to hold up your house. You can't see the wooden studs -- they aren't visible. Finally, you may also have insulation in your walls. This insulation keeps the heat inside your home on a chilly morning or a cold winter night. If you have air conditioning, it also keeps the cool air inside on a hot, summer day.

Your body is a kind of home also. Your skin covers most of your body so we can't actually see what's inside. But what's inside is really extraordinary. You have a heart that never stops beating. You have a brain with 85-90 billion neurons. You have a network of blood vessels that, if laid end to end, would measure about 60,000 miles! You have a nervous system with about 1,300 nerve cells per square inch embedded in your skin. You have over 200 bones. And of course there are many critical organs like your liver and kidney which keep you alive each day. All this, and much more, are inside a body that you think of as "you." All hidden inside the skin.

There's a Japanese word, *okagesama*, which is often used conversationally to express thanks. The root of this word, *kage*, means "shadow." It acknowledges that there are unseen forces in this world which make our life possible. Okagesama is grounded in an awareness of what's inside the walls of our home and what's under the skin of our body. Of course, it goes much further than that, because virtually every aspect of life is supported by unseen forces that include objects, energy, people and even money that makes life possible. These are the elements of our life that are in the shadow, so to see them, we have to look very deeply at our life. *We have to see with more than just our eyes.*

During a Naikan, participants have a chance to reflect on a particular skill, like driving, cooking or playing a musical instrument. They are asked to trace that skill and identify all the unseen forces that made that skill possible for them. When we do this, we may find that it is an endless exercise. It is an investigation that can never be completed.

I play the piano, yet I have never been able to fully comprehend what has made it possible for me to play. My mother encouraged me to take lessons and was always singing and playing music herself, which was inspiring. My father paid for my first piano and would drive me to my lessons and wait for me. My teacher, Mrs. Braverman, provided me with instruction and sheet music. She was able to teach me because she had a teacher when she was younger. The piano itself is an amazing instrument and the process of building a piano is complex and precise. It involves wood, which came from living trees that had to be cut and milled. It has more than 225 strings, which are made from high carbon steel. Each of those strings has to be tuned, regularly, to maintain the piano's lovely sound. The keys themselves are made from wood and plastic. There are people who transported the pianos on which I practiced. There was gas and oil required for my father's car to drive me to lessons. My father received money, from his job at a bakery, in order to pay for my lessons. My hearing allowed me to listen to music so I could learn to play. It goes on and on. Endlessly.

Okagesama is the recognition of these forces that are hidden in the shadow of our lives. Self-reflection allows us to see inside the walls and under the skin of our day-to-day existence. We become aware of how we are supported, cared for, and loved even as we send an email, drink a cup of coffee, or take a shower.

Because something is in a shadow, it does not mean it doesn't exist.

A shadow does not negate the existence of what is hidden. It simply means we can't see it because there is an absence of light. And when we bring the light of awareness to that shadow, what do we find? We often find love? Quiet, inconspicuous, unassuming love. And that love brings a smile to our heart.

Okagesama.

Resources

Also by Gregg Krech

The Art of Taking Action: Lessons from Japanese Psychology

Naikan: Gratitude, Grace, and the Japanese Art of Self-Reflection

A Natural Approach to Mental Wellness: Japanese Psychology and the Skills We Need for Psychological and Spiritual Health

Question Your Life: Naikan Self-Reflection and the Transformation of our Stories

Online Courses

- ❖ A Natural Approach to Mental Wellness
- ❖ Gratitude, Grace & a Month of Self-Reflection
- ❖ Living on Purpose
- ❖ Working with your Attention
- ❖ Taking Action: Finishing the Unfinished (and Unstarted)

Websites

www.todoinstitute.org

www.thirtythousanddays.org

www.artoftakingaction.org

www.distancelearningpsychology.org

Thirty Thousand Days

Thirty Thousand Days is an inspiring (ad-free) quarterly publication. It is a blend of the practical, the psychological and the spiritual and is the only publication of its kind, exploring the relationship between living well and mental health. (free sample issue available)

Made in the USA
Middletown, DE
03 January 2021

30604911R00064